HOW TO
SET UP and MARKET a
FAMILY MEDIATION BUSINESS

# Going
# it Alone

Catherine Frances + Richard Wyatt

First published in Great Britain as a softback original in 2022

Copyright © Catherine Frances and Richard Wyatt

The moral right of this author has been asserted.

Typeset in Palatino

Design, typesetting and publishing by UK Book Publishing

www.ukbookpublishing.com

ISBN: 978-1-915338-00-6

# Going it Alone

The law has recently changed and it is now a legal requirement that all couples who are separating or divorcing attend at least one mediation session. Thus, the numbers of post-graduates training to be mediators is rapidly increasing. All mediators must be registered with the Family Mediation Council (FMC).

It is a requirement of the FMC that 'all family mediators consider how to set up as a mediator and how to obtain clients once trained and registered with the FMC'. However, no such text or guidance exists for family mediators working towards accreditation and registration ... until now!

Richard Wyatt is an experienced marketing consultant, whose work has included advising the FMC. Catherine Frances is a newly registered mediator who has set up her own mediation business.

# Contents

1. Introduction                                                    1

2. Options                                                         3

3. SWOT Analysis
   – Test the viability of your business proposition               5

4. Business plan                                                  11

5. Funding options                                                14

6. Choosing a name                                                20

7. Find a domain name for your business.                          22

8. Register your business with Companies House.                   24

9. Set up a bank account                                          27

10. Payment systems                                               28

11. Professional Indemnity Insurance                              34

12. General Data Protection Regulations 2018                      36

13. Create your own website                                       40

14. Track website behaviour and goals                             48

15. Pictures                                                      51

16. Design a logo                                                 53

17. Finding an office                                          55

18. Tools of the trade                                         59

19. Paperwork                                                  61

20. Letter to participant B                                    63

21. A marketing strategy                                       67

22. Identifying your target audiences &
    working out how best to reach them                         77

23. Getting your message right                                 84

24. Understanding online audiences                            95

25. Finding and nurturing 'third party' referrers            106

26. Using the media                                           109

27. Planning your next steps in 20 minutes                   120

28. Making a FIVE YEAR PLAN                                   123

Appendix I – Business Plan                                    126

Appendix II – Sample Invoice                                  132

About the authors                                             134

# 1.
# Introduction

Taking the plunge to go it alone and start your own mediation business is a giddying, heart-stopping experience. Once you've made this decision you'll face myriad small decisions and numerous variables – from what name to choose through to how to find clients.

It's these decisions which this book aims to help you through. Once you've established yourself this book helps you work out how to market your mediation business in the long-term. This book is specifically written for mediators starting a new venture, or mediators hoping to expand an existing business.

There are numerous links to relevant websites in this book so it would be useful to read it in conjunction with a mobile phone or tablet to hand.

Richard Wyatt has an extensive professional background in campaigns, communications and PR. In this book, Richard brings his expertise to specifically focus on the mediation profession. This will be of interest to new and experienced mediators needing to freshen up their marketing strategy.

Marketing a mediation business takes a special approach, since it is an ongoing activity, as – hopefully – you don't get many repeat clients once they've reached a settlement.

Catherine Frances is a newly minted mediator who set up her own business from scratch, falling into every pitfall on the way! Hopefully this book will help you navigate around the traps and hazards faced by many budding mediator entrepreneurs.

# 2.
# Options

When you complete the Foundation Training Course, you'll be faced with a number of options for progressing your career, up to and beyond accreditation.

## Options

- Go it alone – company director! Complete control and profit but huge responsibility, no-one to bounce ideas off. (The role of your PPC will be especially important.) You'll not only be the MD but the Head of sales and marketing (including social media), Head of operations (customer service and product development) and Head of finance (accounting and HR). Quite a daunting prospect!
- Co-directors – share the load, expense, responsibility and profit. Option to co-mediate, quickly accommodate an influx of clients, and general moral support.

Franchise-style – work as a self-employed mediator for a large organisation, like South West Mediation Ltd or Family Mediation Centre Staffordshire. You set your hours and they provide the work and administrative support. In return you receive a percentage of the client's fees – usually approximately 40%. This model works especially well for online mediation. Although many require mediators to be accredited, some run schemes for those who are working towards accreditation (WTA) and it's always worth an approach, in case you are just what is needed at the particular time[1].

- Join an existing company – opportunities are advertised in the FMC and FMA Newsletters and also Lesley Saunders' Affordable CPD Monthly Bulletin www.affordablecpd.co.uk

This book is mainly aimed at mediators in the first two categories, but hopefully will be of interest to all mediators reviewing their websites and marketing strategies.

---

1   It might be worth considering a hybrid model of part-time franchise-style work for financial stability while setting up your own business.

# 3.
# SWOT Analysis
# – Test the viability of your business proposition

So, you've decided to start a mediation business. The first thing you need to do is identify your strengths and weaknesses, together with external opportunities and threats, in other words, do a SWOT analysis.

SWOT is unique to each business and helps test the viability of a business proposition. SWOT analysis gives you talking points for your business plan and concrete action points for getting launched.

| STRENGTHS Internal Assessment WEAKNESSES | |
| --- | --- |
| What do you do well?<br><br>Internal resources, eg. People, knowledge, background, education, reputation, skills etc.<br><br>Assets eg. Capital, credit, existing customers, patents, technology.<br><br>Advantages over the competition?<br><br>Research and development capabilities?<br><br>Positive aspects that offer a competitive advantage?<br><br>How can you expand on your strengths?<br>Can strengths help deal with threats?<br><br>Can strengths help exploit more opportunities? | What does the business lack?<br><br>What factors are within your control that detract from ability to maintain a competitive edge? What could be better?<br><br>Limited resources?<br><br>Marketing strategy?<br><br>Poor location?<br><br>Which are the most glaring weaknesses?<br><br>Can the weaknesses be fixed?<br><br>Will it take more money, people, knowledge? |

| OPPORTUNITIES External Assessment THREATS | |
|---|---|
| What opportunities exist in your market or environment that you can benefit from?<br><br>What can help the idea 'take off'?<br><br>Is the perception of the business positive?<br><br>Market changes that can create an opportunity?<br><br>Is opportunity ongoing or limited, ie. is timing critical?<br><br>Set goals for each opportunity.<br><br>Ensure goals are SMART*<br><br>Consider 'PESTLE'** | Existing and potential competitors?<br><br>What factors are beyond your control that could put your business at risk?<br><br>Unfavourable trends or developments that may lead to drop in revenue or profit?<br><br>What situations or environment might threaten your market efforts?<br><br>Changes in supplier prices?<br><br>Shifts in consumer behaviour, economy or regulations that could reduce sales?<br><br>Consider 'PESTLE'** |

* SMART = specific, measurable, attainable, relevant and a timeline

**PESTLE = political, economic, sociological, technical, legislative, environmental factors

Threats tend to attack weaknesses first, so use this as another opportunity to remedy your weaknesses and reduce the risk posed by threats. Conversely, strengths can help deal with threats and help exploit or open up more opportunities.

An example of SWOT analysis that enabled Catherine to turn a weakness and threat into a strength that would exploit opportunities is CIM. Mediators cannot do the Child Inclusive Mediation training until they have been accredited for three years, therefore a weakness was the inability to offer CIM, and a threat from competitors who could. The experienced mediator, Margaret Pendlebury, was engaged as a CIM Specialist Advisor instantly turning CIM into a strength that could exploit more CIM opportunities in future cases, eliminating any 'threat'.

To turn the SWOT analysis into strategies, look at the strengths you identified and then come up with ways to use those strengths to maximise opportunities. Then look at how the same strengths can be used to minimise the threats identified. For example, use testimonials from current clients to promote your brand on the website and in online marketing – such as reviews on Google-my-business.

Catherine's SWOT analysis looked something like this:

| STRENGTHS | Internal Assessment | WEAKNESSES |
|---|---|---|
| Qualified<br><br>Experienced<br><br>Priced competitively<br><br>Town-centre office with free parking<br><br>Offer face-to-face and online mediation<br><br>Good PPC | | Relying on one person – lone worker<br><br>No Legal aid or CIM<br><br>No repeat business – constant marketing<br><br>No accounting or marketing experience<br><br>No brand recognition |
| **OPPORTUNITIES** | External Assessment | **THREATS** |
| Changes in law<br><br>Post corona-virus potential to increase work<br><br>Online mediation<br><br>CIM – Child Inclusive Mediation<br><br>Legal Aid clients | | Another lockdown<br><br>Competitors in the market<br><br>Brexit uncertainties |

## Task – write your own SWOT Analysis

| STRENGTHS Internal Assessment WEAKNESSES | |
|---|---|
| | |

| OPPORTUNITIES External Assessment THREATS | |
|---|---|
| | |

You can take SWOT a step further by creating a five year plan at the end of the book.

# 4.
# Business plan

It can be a bit daunting sitting down with a blank sheet of paper to write your business plan, but it need not be a tome (unless you're applying for funding from a bank or investor). However, crafting a business plan will force you to think strategically and methodically through your mediation business proposition. It will compel you to research the competition and identify niches for your business (refer back to your SWOT analysis.) You will quickly draw up basic accounts that will determine your fees and what you need to survive and prosper.

Essentially, your business plan outlines what your business does and what you are trying to achieve. It explains what the market opportunity is, what makes your business special, and how you will make it a success. It should be concise, specific and demonstrate a knowledge of your market and finances. Give it a professional cover, start with an executive summary or business description and include detailed information in an appendix.

Your business plan can form the foundation of your business with written language you can use for marketing and other purposes. For example, you can lift your one minute 'elevator pitch' directly from your 'Company Aim'.

The sample Business Plan included in Appendix I includes the following sections:

- Name
- Companies House Registration Number
- Domain Name
- Company Aim
- Proposed Premises
- Business Description
- Competitive Analysis
    - Strengths
    - Weaknesses

- Development Plan
- Financial Factors
    - Expenses

- Budget Forecast/Projected Financial Statement
- Marketing

This is not an exhaustive list, but is a good starting point if it's your first time writing a business plan.

# TASK: Write your own business plan

*For more guidance on writing a business plan see: www.gov.uk/write-business-plan or crib from Catherine's in the appendix!*

# 5.
# Funding options

Having written a solid business plan – including a projected financial statement or budget forecast - and researched your market, you will have an understanding of how much money you need to secure in order to make your new business a success.

A brief survey shows that a large proportion of mediators are middle-class women (hopefully this will diversify with time) who can self-finance their business, but if you aren't in this position think laterally and perhaps be prepared to swallow your pride. Funding options range from a bank loan to crowd funding; here we consider a few options in no particular order.

## Bank Loans

A bank loan is the traditional method for securing small business funding but banks can have a high benchmark for applicants, as they need to ensure the business will succeed to recoup their investment plus interest. If you have a high FICO[2] credit score, collateral and possibly some previous business experience you will have a much higher chance of getting a loan than those who don't. Fortunately, many other types of funding exist.

## Personal Investment

Over 90% of start-ups are self-funded, with entrepreneurs using money from their own savings or retirement account. The advantage of personally investing is that you don't have to give up any equity and retain complete control over your business.

## HELOC - Home equity line of credit

Equity release from your home is a commonly advertised method of raising cash for a project. A HELOC has no restrictions on what it can be used for, so could be used to finance a small business. You'll still need to make monthly repayments, even though technically it's *your* money, but a HELOC may have a lower rate of interest than other lines of credit.

---

2   FICO = Fair Isaac Corporation. Fico scores take into account payment history, current level of indebtedness, types of credit used, length of credit history and new credit accounts to determine creditworthiness. Scores in the 670 - 739 range are considered to be 'good' credit history.

## Professional investors

Investors, also known as venture capitalists, are wealthy individuals or businesses prepared to fund promising small businesses – similar to the Dragons on 'Dragons Den'. They will have exacting standards and will expect a portion of the business equity and control in return for their investment.

## Promissory Note

You may be lucky enough to have family or friends who are willing to invest in your venture. To avoid this affecting personal relationships you should draw up a Promissory Note that describes your intention to pay the person back by a certain time and with a certain amount of interest. A promissory note is legally binding.

## Grants

The obvious advantage with a grant is that, unlike a loan, it doesn't have to be repaid.  The skill with grants is knowing where to look for them. They are often targeted at specific individuals or types of business, eg. women, immigrants, scientific research and development, social or environmental benefits or residents of a particular area, and so on. Contact your local Chamber of Commerce for leads to grants (and loans) or search for local charitable trusts, like the Barnwood

Trust who fund individuals with ideas that will benefit residents in Gloucestershire[3].

# Business Credit Cards

Applying for a credit card is relatively straightforward, in that you don't need a business plan and it makes sense for sole proprietors or self-employed mediators. 0% credit cards can be effective for launching a small business provided you repay at least the monthly minimum and aim to clear the card within the 0% interest period[4]. See https://www.money.co.uk/credit-cards.htm or check Martin Lewis' guide to cards offering 0% interest for a number of months.

# Government Assistance

First check: **https://www.gov.uk/business-finance-support**

Contact your local authority for details of discretionary business grants and start-up loans. And don't forget to apply for reduction in business rates while you're there. The local Chamber of Commerce might be able to direct you to local grants and loans.

---

3    The Barnwood Trust helped fund my Foundation Training.
4    Martin Lewis recommends dividing what you spent by the number of 0% months and setting up a direct debit to clear it in that time, so it works like a loan where you pay it back in full over a set period.

# Crowdfunding

This is a relatively new way of raising funds for good causes and businesses online. It is inexpensive and easy to set up a crowdfunding platform like Kickstarter or Indiegogo; supporters give a cash donation, some in exchange for rewards or equity. Crowdfunding platforms work best if used in conjunction with a website to promote your idea or business to potential investors. How successful this would be for a mediation business is debateable.

# Universal Credit

There is some stigma attached to 'signing on' for Universal Credit, however no-one knows unless you tell them! If you are starting out from scratch, UC can support your family financially for the first year of your start-up business, relieving you from the pressure of turning enough profit to provide an income from the start. It also means that what profit you do make can be spent on training and your PPC and getting accredited![5]

# Business Competitions

If you are confident you have the charisma to promote your mediation practice, then entering a business competition can raise the profile of your company and there is often prize

---

5    The FMA has a discretionary fund that can assist mediators on benefits with their annual membership fees.

money attached; but obviously this should be as a bonus rather than your main finance strategy.

## Re-investing Profits

Regardless of how you finance your business, you should create a plan for re-investing a percentage of profits back into your mediation practice. This can help you focus on marketing and advertising, expanding to a new location or taking on an administrator or additional mediator – or achieving whatever else you put in your three and five year plans.

## Covid-19

If Covid-19 continues to affect businesses, central government will continue to provide funding, distributed through local authorities which business owners can apply for. Contact your local council for details about the various discretionary support schemes. The schemes vary according to the lockdown period and whether a business was open or closed; either way you will probably have to show the pandemic has had a negative impact on your business.

# 6.
# Choosing a name

Choosing a name needs to be done in conjunction with checking the URL is available and the name isn't already listed with Companies House.

Many people choose their surname or location + 'family mediation', Like Anna Vollans' 'Vollans Mediation' and Lesley Allport's 'Lesley Allport Dispute Resolution'. Although using your name makes you sound like a smaller organisation, it has more 'personal' connotations and is especially useful if you already have a network of contacts - like solicitors - and an established reputation.

Using your town or city name has the benefit of sounding like a grander business, and you can use the royal 'We'! Many people Google 'mediation + town name' so using the location name can help you pick up *ad hoc* business, especially in your first few months, particularly for clients seeking face-to-face mediation. It also makes it easier to expand and employ co-mediators and colleagues than under one person's name. But this could geographically restrict your audience in a time of unrestricted Zoom mediation.

The other choice is a 'meaningful' name which conjures up desirable images, such as Venetia Tosswell's 'True North Mediation' or Devorah Greenberg's 'Sage Mediation'.

**Other things to consider when choosing a name include:**

- Is the name original and unique? (Availability will be discussed in Domain Names.)
- Searchable, memorable, easy to spell and say.
- Raise any trademark issues, for example if your name happens to be Honda or Toyota.
- Mean something unfortunate in a different language[6].
- Work with the company's mission statement and values
- Is it appropriate within the market?
- What image does the name conjure up? Clear aim and purpose, professional, trustworthy, distinguished, specialist, prestigious?

---

6    For example, the Vauxhall 'Nova' car translates as 'no go' in Spanish.

# 7.
# Find a domain name for your business

An internet domain name is the unique name of an organization or person on the Internet. The name is combined with a generic top-level domain, such as .com and .gov. Anyone can use .com .org .net but some, like .edu .gov .mil are restricted. Sponsored links include: .toshiba .vacations .jobs Every country has a top-level domain for example .uk .ca (Canada) .jp (Japan).

By 2019 there were more than 300 million registered domain names. In order for the domain name to be visible on the Internet, it must first be registered with any one of the 'registrars' eg. GoDaddy, 123Reg etc. (Google 'domain name registrars' for more options.) A registrar is a company that takes your domain registration information and reserves your domain from the main registry. Registrars vary in price, services offered (eg. support by phone, email or chat), terms, ease of use, management system, etc. but choose one that is ICANN accredited. It usually takes about 48 hours to register a domain name.

We're assuming here that you will want your company name in your domain name, to make it easier for customers to find you on the internet. You will probably want to choose between .com for global appeal or .co.uk to attract UK business. But there is nothing to stop you purchasing multiple domains; for example, strafordfamilymediation.co.uk/.com/.org /.net

If you make your website using Weebly.com you can get a free domain name, although it will have 'Weebly' in the domain name, eg. stratfordfamilymediation.weebly.com

You'll find many mediation names are already taken. If your preferred domain name is not available, try adding a prefix such as 'My' or 'The'[7] or suffix 'Practice', 'Centre' or 'Dispute Resolution'. Make sure it can be verbally communicated, without having to be spelt out each time and can quickly be typed without error eg. my surname 'frances' is generally spelt 'francis' and would be crying out for input mistakes! Try not to choose a name that is too long to remember. eg The Plymouth and District Family Mediation Practice – even 'tpadfmp' would be tricky to remember and prone to errors.

If you use a generic domain name your image will not be as strong as having a custom domain name. eg cathy@gmail.com Vs cathy@stratfordfamilymediation.com although the former may be free.

---

7   'The FMA' distinguishes the Family Mediators Association from other 'FMAs' on the internet.

# 8.
# Register your business with Companies House

Before you register your domain name check the name is also available with Companies House.

Google 'companies house name check'.

Don't mistakenly use a formation agent to register your company - like I did - thinking it would make the registration process easier. This is only necessary for overseas companies who need a UK Head Office address for registration purposes.

You'll be given the choice of setting up as a sole trader or a limited company.

You need to set up as a sole trader if any of the following apply: you earned more than £1,000 from self-employment in the fiscal year running from April to April; you need to prove you're self-employed, for example to claim Tax-Free Childcare; you want to make voluntary Class 2 National Insurance payments to help you qualify for benefits.

A limited company is a company 'limited by shares' or 'limited by guarantee'

Limited by shares companies are usually businesses that make a profit. This means the company:

- is legally separate from the people who run it
- has separate finances from your personal ones
- has shares and shareholders
- can keep any profits it makes after paying tax.

Limited by guarantee companies are usually 'not for profit'. This means the company:

- is legally separate from the people who run it
- has separate finances from your personal ones
- has guarantors and a 'guaranteed amount'
- invests profits it makes back into the company.

To summarize, you will probably want to register as the Director of a company that is limited by shares, even if you are the only shareholder.

Note that when you open a bank account they will require the account holder's address to be the same as that shown on the Companies House Certificate. If in any doubt about where you'll be operating from or if you may use several locations, it is easiest to use your home address as the Head Office for your company. It is relatively simple to change the address at a later date. One thing to note is that Companies House records are public, so the address will be freely searchable, ie. don't use your home address if this will cause you problems in another area of your life, for example, if you also work as a social worker.

Keep a record of your Company Number *and* your Company Authentication Code (which doesn't change) as you'll need both of these in all your communications with Companies House.

Every year you will be asked to submit an online Confirmation Statement confirming that your company is still in business, otherwise you will be 'struck off' the register. You'll receive a reminder letter about when to do this. The current fee is £13[8].

---

8   As of May 2021

# 9.
# Set up a bank account

If you have registered with Companies House as a Sole Trader there is no legal requirement to have a business bank account – although financial advisors still recommend that you do. Limited Companies must have a business bank account.

There are a bewildering range of business bank accounts on offer, many offering free banking for the first 18 months; others like TSB offer free Square Readers for debit and credit cards. Also compare the cost of transaction fees especially for card payments. For the best objective (un-sponsored) comparison of business bank accounts Google 'Which? Compare business accounts'.

Some financial advisors recommend having a second account for accumulating the 20% (or more) tax that will have to be paid the following year.

Remember that the address you use for the bank account must be the same as that shown as the Head Office on the Companies House Certificate. Both the bank and Companies House will accept your home address as the Head Office.

# 10.
# Payment systems

A payment system is any system used to settle financial transactions through the transfer of monetary value using debit or credit cards.

The use of cash declined by 27% between 2007 (61%) and 2017 (34%), but occasionally a client will pay in cash at the end of a session. BACS transfer payments direct to your bank account on receipt of an invoice rely on the honesty of the client to honour the payment, ie. if the outcome of the mediation session is unsuccessful the client might not feel inclined to pay. (See Appendix II for a sample invoice.)

According to UK Finance[9] debit and credit cards were used to make 16.3 billion payments in the UK in 2017, estimated to rise to 23.6 billion by 2027. Today 98% of the population hold a debit card and 60% a credit card, so obviously you want to offer your clients the option of paying by card because if you don't your competitors certainly will!  It also makes your business appear efficient, legitimate and contemporary. Ideally, clients

---

9   The bank industry's trade body

should pay *before* their mediation session, with the obvious advantages of getting payment out of the way and reducing the chance of a no-show. You will, however, need to consider a cancellation/refund policy.

There are two ways to process card payments: electronically through swipe or contactless POS (Point of Sale) payment gateways or through manual keyed entry CNP (Card Not Present) payment gateways.

## POS – Point of Sale – Payment Gateways

POS terminals are where the client inserts their card with a pin or contactless, like at supermarket checkouts. They are typically managed by a third party and make their profit by charging a small percentage of every transaction.

Every payment gateway provider has their own terms of use and fees. Usually, you will have a gateway setup fee, monthly gateway fee, merchant account setup, and a fee for each transaction processed. Read all the pricing documentation to avoid hidden fees or additional expenses.

For example: SumUp has the lowest transaction fees (1.69%) and no paperwork; Square card machine only costs £19 – or is provided free by some banks – eg. with a TSB Business Account. iZettle is 25% faster than its competitors (contactless payments are approved in seconds) and can be used with hardware like a receipt printer or barcode reader.

POS systems a reasonably secure against fraud but involve payment at the time of the mediation session and, as mentioned before, the possibility of no shows.

# CNP – Card Not Present – Payment Gateways

CNP Payment Gateways are an online or telephone payment system that allows you to securely and conveniently accept payments without a card reader or the card/card holder being present. They are also called 'virtual terminal', 'MOTO' (Mail Order/Telephone Order) or eCommerce transactions.

It is useful to choose a provider that is able to support you in meeting the strict Payment Card Industry Data Security Standard (PCI DSS) compliance rules protecting your business and clients, since CNP (especially telephone) payments are vulnerable to fraud. Sometimes protection is included in the monthly fee and others require you to complete an annual PCI self-assessment questionnaire.

## Telephone CNP Payment Gateways

These are useful if you have an administrator who can take payment over the phone at the time of booking an appointment. Many POS systems also allow you to key in CNP card details.

# Internet CNP Payment Gateways

There are two types of internet CNP payment gateways; hosted and integrated.

'Hosted' means that clients are directed away from your website to a hosted gateway portal on another site, for example Paypal, Barclaycard Business or Worldpay. The advantages are that clients will probably be familiar with the hosted site and feel more confident entering their card details into the site. They will also take care of compliance with PCI DSS when handling confidential data, and it may be easier to set up than integrating a payment system into your website.  The payment method can be included on a website as a discrete page, that isn't openly available for guests to view, but a link to the page can be sent to clients for payment.

Disadvantages include that they tend to be more expensive to run and clients are directed away from your website.

They charge a variety of fees; some charge an initial signup fee plus a transaction fee, while others are free only charging a transaction fee. You want to create a seamless, simple, hassle-free process for your customers, as the check-out is the point where the majority of customers abandon their booking.

When choosing a hosted gateway, you want to evaluate the overall cost to your business. It may be tempting to choose the system with the cheapest monthly and transaction fees, but also consider those that offer PCI DSS compliance, tech support and smooth method of connecting to your website.

For example: Square has no contract or monthly fees but a 2.5% card rate. Worldpay charges £9.95+ monthly fees and has different contracts and card rates subject to turnover and card type. PayPal has a 2% + 30p per transaction charge but no monthly fee, so they only make money if you make money. SagePay has a £15+ monthly fee; different contract options and card rates are negotiable. SumUp is subject to application and approval.

Details of the best online payment systems, their fees, pros and cons are detailed at:

https://www.cardswitcher.co.uk/online-payment-systems/

## Integrated CNP payment systems

This means the payment system is an integral part of your website, so clients do not leave your site to make a payment.

John Cleary helped set up a slick integrated booking system using Calendly online calendar linked to the 'Call to action' ('Contact us' 'Book an appointment now') on Catherine's website. Potential clients can in theory book a MIAM or mediation session at a mutually convenient time on the Calendly available dates and times, then pay by card or Baccs to confirm the booking. The drawback to this is we haven't managed to set it up for two people to book and pay for the same mediation session, so this needs some work. (Answers on a postcard please!)[10]

Whichever system you choose John Rohn[11] recommends you 'Earn as much money as you possibly can and as quickly as you can. The sooner you get money out of the way, the sooner you will be able to get to the rest of your problems in style'.

# 11.
# Professional Indemnity Insurance

Professional indemnity insurance is an important type of business insurance if you give advice, provide a professional service to clients, or handle other people's data or intellectual property. So most professionals such as architects, engineers, accountants and mediators need PII. It protects you from mistakes you make at work that result in a financial loss to your client, specifically after you've provided them with a service or advice, and covers legal fees and compensation payments.

Insurance coverage generally starts from £50,000 and can go as high as £5,000,000. It's important for you to determine your own level of risk. One rule of thumb is to think how much it would cost to financially pay back your client if you make a mistake.

Not all insurance companies recognise 'mediators' as a profession for PII purposes. The following insurance companies are among the few who do provide PII for mediators:

- Towergate: www.towergateinsurance.co.uk/counsellors-insurance
- Howdens: www.howdengroup.com
- Oxygen : www.marshcommercial.co.uk/for-business/oxygen/
- Holistic : www.holisticinsurance.co.uk/
- Balens: www.balens.co.uk/
- Hiscox: www.hiscox.co.uk/
- PPS: www.ppstrust.org/

'Aggregate' policies, where you can have multiple claims within your limit, eg £2m in totality, are - obviously - cheaper than 'one claim' policies where you can have multiple claims each up to your limit, eg £2m each.

We were shocked at the range of quotes for the same cover, so recommend shopping around and querying renewal quotes.

You may also wish to consider Public Liability insurance that generally covers everything to do with the public and Employers Liability insurance if you are hiring people.

# 12.
# General Data Protection Regulations 2018

The GDPR applies to 'personal data' and defines this as 'any information relating to an identifiable person who can be directly or indirectly identified in particular by reference to an identifier'. This includes things like names and addresses, phone numbers and email addresses, bank and credit card details, and internet provider (IP) address. Mediators also keep information about current and historical circumstances and events, children, court orders, etc. and we need to be duly respectful of our clients' right to privacy and protect their personal information as we would like our own protected.

As a self-employed mediator you are classed as a 'Data Controller' under GDPR and you need to register with the Information Commissioner's Office (ICO). You can register at:

https://ico.org.uk/registration/new

The registration fee is £40[12]. 'Mediator' is not specifically listed as a profession[13] so maybe follow the 'Legal' .... 'other legal professional' route to register.

There are six lawful reasons for collecting personal data of which three apply to mediation:

- Consent – where the individual has given clear consent for you to process their data.
- Legitimate interest – where the processing is necessary for the legitimate interests of either the controller or a third party.
- Contract – where processing is necessary for a contract you have with the individual or they have asked you to take specific steps before entering into a contract (eg. legal aid).

Clients have a right to be informed, right to access, right to erasure and right to withdraw consent. Here, it is useful to quote Lesley Saunders on how GDPR relates to mediation.

"As a mediator myself I am aware that I start out in a MIAM with referral information that I might not need and with a MIAM record asking for information that will cover everything in the eventuality of having to write an MOU. So, we need to be thinking about that. If there is a child case, do we really need to know and record if or when they were married or divorced? Whether and when they lived together? Do we need to know (outside the legal aid contract) the

---

12  2021 price
13  Although 'Slimming World Consultant' is?!

parents' dates of birth? Or the children's (although we do need to know their ages)? Clearly there are things that are helpful – if someone has mobility issues we need to know to provide an appropriate service, we might also need to make adjustments around other (mental) health issues. Ethnicity is helpful if we are working to ensure that we meet the needs of local communities, but outside of the legal aid agency, I have never known a service to actually use the information to target marketing. If we have a property and finance case do we need to know about children if they are not dependent? These are the kinds of questions we need to be asking ourselves about the information we collect. The answer is not necessarily to have a form of every eventuality but to be clear at referral that we record only the essential information to be able to accept and progress the case, be that in relation to the client or third parties; and with mediators that in their work they record only the information appropriate to that particular case.

"Sharing is mostly going to be with mediators (including trainees) and clients, sometimes PPCs and occasionally other services such as children's services. Again, clarity is the watchword here."

Sharing should be done securely. Data should be kept as long as makes sense, is reasonable, do-able and explicit. Disposable should be by cross-shredder[14] or secure disposal service; electronic data deleted and the trash emptied.

---

14 "... old fashioned shredders that convert paper into long strips that someone can tape together to access the information (I know it sounds absurd but it has been done), are no longer acceptable." Lesley Saunders

We're human so errors and breaches can occur. The ICO website has information on how to deal with this and detailed general guidance on GDPR: http://ico.org.uk/for-organisation/

# 13.
# Create your own website[15]

There are many reasons for having a website, including:

- First impression of a professional business
- Public profile
- Project brand - Company image, personality, professional, polished
- Trust and credibility (permanent)
- Content is evergreen – always there not transient
- Contactable – call to action/bookings
- Additional information and details
- Advertise services and products
- Testimonials
- Marketing tool for exposure
- Breaking geographical barriers – global potential! (Especially with Zoom.)

---

15 The FMA Member's Website also provides information on 'How to write a website'

- You own it! (Other platforms are rented.) And you own the layout
- Essential to have an online presence these days.

If you're a computer whizz and can make your own website, then please do. Top website builders include: WIX.com, Weebly, Squarespace, Webnode, Jimdo, duda, GoDaddy and WordPress.com. Many have free templates for you to use, then you pay for upgrades or additional features.

Catherine, on the other hand, wasted many hair-pulling hours on some of these sites before finally deferring to a private marketing expert; in this case St Pauls Marketing Consultancy[16] who for £1,000[17] built and populated a website and provided three smart logo options. We agreed a price which tailored to the site contents and agreed a timescale for going live. All developers should provide you with an outline costed proposal so you can choose between them. We've provided our experience as a guide, but quotes from three companies will usually give you a reasonable benchmark.

Look at competitor's websites to see what appeals to you and what doesn't, and let your web designer know which features you like or dislike in terms of imagery, language, tone or design style.

The minimum pages you will probably require are:

- Homepage

---

16  www.stpaulsmarketing.co.uk  Tel 0121 293 1197

17  March 2021 price

- About Us
- Services – Mediation
- News – Blog, Twitter, etc.
- Contact Us

Many also have a 'Useful Information' page, but the more pages you have, the more expensive it is to set up.

It is vital that your website developer understands mediation, ie. what you do and what you want to achieve. Many hours were spent in consultation with St Pauls.

Will potential clients have been referred to you? Be hoping to learn more about mediation? Want to learn more about you and your practice? Either way, you want to attract and appeal to your ICA.

Ideal Client Avatar (or ICA) is what marketing experts call your client or target audience. Your ICA won't be children or singles, probably not domestic violence or abuse cases, nor anything related to unlawful activities. It might be separating or divorcing couples, solicitors, parents and homeowners. Make it easy for them to find the information they need quickly and easily. Try to establish a connection with visitors. Answer your ICA's questions 'How? What? Where? When? Why? Who? Can I? Do I?' and you'll be viewed as an authority in your field.

But don't be too creative with navigation. The door handle is where it is for a reason!

Refer back to your strengths in the SWOT analysis and promote these. For example, are you CIM trained? A PPC? Have a legal aid contract? Offering mediation by Zoom is almost a given these days!

Whether to include prices on your homepage? St Pauls put them at the bottom of the 'About' page, but maybe they should have been placed more prominently on a 'costs' page ... or would that deter clients? We suggest you look at competitor's websites and decide.

There are endless mediation websites for you to peruse and glean ideas from; however, there are a few basic rules regarding content to optimise readability:

Ensure your website is mobile-friendly; 80% of websites were viewed on phones in 2020. According to Margin Media, 52% of users said they would be less likely to engage with a company if their mobile experience on the site was bad. And 48% said that if they arrive on a site that isn't working well on their mobile, they take it as an indication that the business doesn't care. Econsultancy found that 62% of companies that designed a website specifically for mobile users had increased sales.

Consider the tone of the website: educational, humorous, 1st person, 3rd person? A mediation website probably wants to be informative and serious yet warm and human (remembering that 'people buy from people'.) Aim to educate and inform rather than sell your service; position yourself and your content in a way that establishes you as a leader in your field, providing useful information. Use the active, rather than the passive voice; eg. 'You can contact us ...' rather than 'we can be contacted …' Even the imperative inviting the reader to 'contact us' with a hyperlink to your contact page is succinct and fine. Website readers have a short attention span so put the most important information at the top. Sentences should not be more than 35 words long. Use strong verbs and simple sentence construction, in other words, conversational English. Personalise the message and reach out to your ICA target audience. Try to explain how the reader will really benefit from mediation, in other words, don't write from the perspective of the mediator, but from the perspective of a prospective client asking 'How will I benefit from mediation?' Sell the sizzle, not the steak!

Make the pages easy to scan for information by using lists or bullet points; organise the content into labelled tabs or sections, eg. How does mediation work? What can I expect? What do I do next? Also include plenty of white space around photos and text.

Don't forget to include:

- A strong 'call to action' - marketing-speak for 'Contact' - invite the viewer to seek more information on every page – 'Contact us!' Make it easy for visitors to contact you. At first contact you probably only need their email address, telephone number and short message. A long questionnaire asking for their solicitor's details and NI number might put off potential clients.
- A map and directions.

- FMC and member organisation logos – Family Mediators Association, College of Mediators, Resolution and National Family Mediation.
- Your PPC as a 'consultant advisor'.
- All the testimonials you have! Show, don't tell.
- Multimedia – a picture, a video or infographic. Research has shown that 90% of information transmitted to the brain is visual, and visual information is processed 60,000 times faster than text.
- Subtitles: 80% of videos are watched with the sound down so subtitles are essential.
- Existing marketing materials, pictures and logos. Conversely, mirror the website pictures and logo in marketing materials. See 'Pictures' below for image sources.

Avoid:

- Jargon, like MIAM and CIM without explanation. Your website is for everyone, not just mediation experts.
- Directing ICAs away from your website. Layer your website content by creating hyperlinks to specific words or phrases to other relevant places within your site. Although you can link to external websites, like Citizen's Advice, this is encouraging people to leave your website, which is not desirable! Note that St Paul's have added CAB as an 'Important Link' at the bottom of Stratford Family Mediation website pages.

Don't forget SEO – good Search Engine Optimisation practices can drive quality traffic to your website. These include focusing on one keyword or phrase per page, including the key word in the title, headings, page URL, throughout the content, in metatags (title and description), image file names and alt tags, and hyperlinks. In our case 'mediation' is probably our SEO keyword phrase. (More about this in Chapter 24.)

The FMA 'How to write a website brief' suggests using the following headings as a guide to providing a developer with the information they will need to construct a website for you:

- Background/context/reasons for creating/updating the website
- About (you and your company)
- Aims of the website
- Target audiences
- Key messages for each audience
- Key reasons for people to use the website
- Elements/site functionality you know you want
- Existing website/marketing materials
- Budget
- Timescales
- Next steps and contact for questions about the brief.

The majority of websites are Content Management Systems (CMS) which are easier to use and give you the flexibility to make quick and easy changes to the site content – add or delete pages, upload content or images, etc. but major changes need to be made by the developer.

At the contract stage it is useful to clarify what elements you will be able to change and what elements they will change. For example, you will (obviously) want to be able to update the blog, but other elements the developer might amend.

Most importantly, keep your website up to date and current. Use a blog to aid SEO and keep the content fresh.

# 14.
# Track website behaviour and goals

## Set up a Google account

## Google Analytics

You must use Analytics if you have a website. You really must! It is worth spending time exploring its features because it gives you vital information about the way your website is used and what users do when they're there. For example, you can find out:

- How many people visited your site in a period you define, and that you can change
- How many of your web pages were viewed in a given period
- Easy comparisons of data between different periods
- How users found you; which websites referred them to you from a link to you on their site
- What page they 'landed' on

- Which of your pages is most popular
- Whether web visitors were entirely new users, or returning visitors
- What device they were using, for example mobile phones or desktop PCs
- And lots, lots more.

## Search engine optimisation

Search engine optimisation (SEO) has become an industry in itself. Rightly so, because it can be very important indeed. SEO is a way of making sure you are appearing in web searches as high as possible up the list that appears from a web user's search. There are entire books and training courses dedicated to it.

Unless you are completely brilliant at understanding the way search engines respond to search enquiries (in which case why are you reading this!?) you are likely to find outsourcing some basic SEO work to a specialist to be most effective for you, rather than trying it yourself. You'll notice this is the only part of this book that advises getting more specialist help[18]: Everything else here you can do yourself.

**Google my business** – a must for every business! Free business listing to drive customer engagement on Google. Periodically they send an email to say how many times you were viewed, visits to your website and photo views. Useful and free

---

18  SEO is a vital part of website development that can be outsourced

marketing tool. Get clients to leave comments on Google to get a Five Star rating.

**Google Ads** – online advertising, click per view

These are discussed in more detail in Chapter 25 Understanding Online Audiences.

# 15.
# Pictures

## Professional photographs

'People buy from people' so it is best to include a portrait photograph of yourself on your website. Get a professional high resolution photograph – that looks like you *today*. You should be able to get four images for about £200. Wear something bright or have a bright background so your picture stands out on social media like LinkedIn, and to use the same image for all social media platforms for familiarity and consistency. Look for a photographer who specialises in Personal Brand photography[19].

You will also probably want some generic photographs to illustrate your website. You can, of course, take your own original pictures – most phone cameras are high definition. Or for free stock, copyright-free images try the following sites:

---

19 For example, John Cleary in the Midlands www.johnclearyphotography. co.uk

- PEXELS
- Pixabay.com
- UNsplash.com
- Freeimages.com
- Canva
- Pixabay

# 16.
# Design a logo

Your logo will appear everywhere from business cards, letterheads and invoices to website, social media, flyers, signage and branded gifts like pens, mugs and calendars.

Consistency is the key. The logo should be simple, scalable small to large, memorable, impactful, versatile and relevant. A single colour is cheaper to print. A vector file is clearer than pixel files for scaling up.

For complete versatility, you will need your logo in several formats:

- Print format - for letterheads, etc.
- Social format - for social media like LinkedIn
- Vector format – for editing with Adobe Illustrator
- web format – web-enabled format
- colour and black and white.

Check www.bbc.co.uk/copyrightaware or www.gov.uk/howtotrademark to ensure originality.

Google 'logo creator' for online sites that can help you create a logo.

If you need professional help to create a logo, ask your website designer or contact a professional like Joyous Creative.

# 17.
# Finding an office

The options are to:

- Work from home
- Rent a permanent office
- Rent a space (hot-desking or *ad hoc* room rental)

**Work from Home:** Do you even need an office if you're going to do all your work on Zoom? Obviously, this is the cheapest option, provided you can keep up a professional appearance. Actors always warn about the dangers of performing with children and animals!

## ZOOM

At this point it is probably useful to consider how to look good on Zoom. Experts recommend placing the camera as near to eye-height as possible[20] and having natural or artificial light

---

20 Especially important for phones which have wide-angle lenses so distort perspective. Elevate a phone or laptop with a stand.

(a ring light or lamp with a daylight or bright-white LED bulb) *behind the screen* to ensure even lighting[21]. Light from the side will cause shadows. To look attentive, sit square-on to the screen and speak directly to the camera, like a newsreader. In 'gallery view' you can 'click and drag' a speaker's window near to the camera to maintain good eye contact. Tilt your head to one side to emphasise the impression you're listening.

In 'Video settings' you can 'touch up my appearance' and adjust your appearance with 'background and filters'.

To prevent glare off the screen or from background lighting, adjust the light behind the screen slightly above eyelevel and/or get an anti-glare coating on your glasses.

You might consider getting a virtual background made with your logo on it to disguise your kitchen or wherever you Zoom from or avoid distractions in the background. Gus Bhandall the Marketing Guru[22] designed one for £15.

**STRATFORD** FAMILY MEDIATION

www.STRATFORDFAMILYMEDIATION.com

[in]

---

21  Catherine used a soft lighting bulb for a while and looked like she'd just stepped out of a sauna!
22  Contact Gus on LinkedIn (March 2021 price)

Ironically[23], you will need a green screen background to use this – or indeed any – virtual background. You can get sheets of green muslin from £12 which you can pin on the wall behind you through to full scale photographic studio-style screens on stands (£60 - £150). The Eva Tech Chromakey screen which Velcro's onto a chair is easy to use and versatile (from £60 on Amazon). It folds away in its own carrycase when not needed.

**Rent a permanent space**: If you like the discipline of going to work in an office and also want a meeting room to do face-to-face mediation (Covid-permitting), try looking at local authority-owned office premises. They are often serviced - have a reception and receptionist - are furnished, inclusive of all utilities and reasonably priced. They often also provide access to a meeting or conference room. They are generally located near town centres with nearby parking. The local Chamber of Commerce is another good starting place to find out about local office space.

There are several advantages of a permanent office: you have a professional address for correspondence. You can 'set up' the meeting room as appropriate for your mediation style. You can display your professional credentials on the wall. But you do need to ensure you at least cover your rent every month.

**Rent a space:** Versatile, in that you can rent rooms in various locations within your region for face-to-face meetings, and only have to pay when you need the space. This takes a degree of organisation, not just booking the rooms but also having

---

23 Like the Pam Ayres rhyme 'And you can win a goldfish in a plastic bag for free, but the bag has got a hole in and the bowls are fifty p!'

all the relevant paperwork with you and tools of the trade in a portable form. (See below). You also have less control over the suitability of the room for mediation – a round table, not to mention space for 2m social distancing.

Many community centres, holistic centres, town council buildings, etc. will rent out rooms by the hour. Also look for premises offering 'hot desking' facilities as they generally have private meeting and conference rooms you can hire for a reasonable price.

# 18.
# Tools of the trade

## White Board

An essential tool of the Mediator! Conventional flipchart easels cost £140 to £500 then you have the ongoing cost of paper – starting at £18 per A1 pad – but flipchart notes are a permanent record that can be filed with the client's other documents.

If you are going to be operating out of the same place maybe consider a conventional white board or a cheaper alternative, like a 'Dry Erase Film' – a giant wipe-able whiteboard post-it-note, that comes in various sizes and sticks to the wall – but removes just like a Post-it note. A 609 x 904mm one starts at £31 + VAT[24].

---

24  from https://www.officeproducts.co.uk/

If money is no object you could get a Samsung Interactive Display - like used on CSI! – the WMR Series 55" costs £1,729[25], but it is available in different sizes and in monthly instalments.

If you're going to be travelling between venues, you might consider a magnetic desktop easel with a B1 flip pad that comes in its own carry case (from £158.00). Paul Kemp uses Magic Whiteboard Reuseable Sheets that stick to any surface; a roll of 25 perforated sheets costs approximately £30.00 on Amazon.

- **Printer – possibly a portable printer**
- **White board or flipchart pens**
- **Bottled water for clients**
- **Box of tissues**
- **Card machine for taking payments**

---

25 https://samsung.cinos.net/a/samsung-flip-2/?gclid=CjwKCAiA-_L9BRBQEiwA-bm5fsUOkIAF7SaAFliFopcgU6G09CITD2-Julx5w4Ag4lrzLVKIFMU94BoCfE4QAvD_BwE

# 19.
# Paperwork

You will probably already have sample documents from your Foundation Training, including:

- Agreement to mediate
- Agreement to mediate explanatory notes
- Client information form
- Financial disclosure booklet
- Monthly outgoings expenditure schedule
- Open financial summary
- Confidential summary of proposals/MOU
- CIM Consent form for parents

Check the Member's section of your FMC Member Organisation – ie. Family Mediators Association, College of Mediators, Resolution or National Family Mediation for pro formas. After this you will have to prepare everything yourself.

# Other paperwork

Other documents you may need to prepare include the following:

- Telephone message form
- Screening form[26]
- Mediation summary
- Post mediation session letter
- Invoice[27]
- Letter to participant B or 2

Each practice and PPC has their own preferred format for the Mediation Summary and Post Mediation Session letter and you'll be taught these as part of the accreditation process as they are a requirement of the portfolio.

By far the trickiest letter to compose is the letter to Participant B or Participant 2, so we will give this special consideration in the next chapter.

---

26  See Paul kemp's screening form included in Appendix D of Lisa Parkinson's 'Family Mediation' book

27  Example included in Appendix II

# 20.
# Letter to participant B

The most challenging letter you will probably have to compose is the 'out of the blue' letter to participant B. After several attempts at reinventing the wheel, Lisa Parkinson and Lesley Saunders were asked for advice. And it transpires there are several interesting approaches you can take.

On pages 75-76 of her book 'Family Mediation'[28] Lisa writes:

*If Party A is willing to take part, the mediator needs to contact Party B (if not contacted previously) to offer a similar information and assessment meeting. 'B' may imagine that the mediator will be biased after hearing A's side of the story and the offer of a meeting may be declined or ignored. The approach to 'B' should be discussed with 'A', who may say that any suggestion they make to 'B' will be rejected and the approach needs to come from the mediator. In this case, the mediator's letter to 'B' needs to be carefully worded, emphasising the wish to help both (or all) participants equally and, where children are concerned, with a special focus on their needs and well-being. If, on the other hand, 'A' thinks it would be preferable to approach 'B'*

---

28  Lisa Parkinson (2020) 'Family Mediation' LexisNexis

*themselves, emphasising their aim to settle matters by agreement if possible, it may be helpful for the mediator to offer a draft letter for 'A' to personalise and send to 'B'. Mediators need to use empathy, strategic thinking and skills to reach out to and engage both parties. Experience suggests that a careful approach can result in nearly all 'B's attending an initial meeting, with far greater opportunities for mediation than if only 'A' attends. Mediators' time and skills are not well used if they undertake initial meetings with one party alone, without the other party receiving similar information and understanding how mediation could help them and the family as a whole.*

In private correspondence Lisa wrote: '*So I think the mediator should discuss with A, probably on the phone, whether B should be contacted before A is offered a MIAM and if so, whether by A or by the mediator - or only after A has attended a MIAM, explained the issues and considered how to approach B.*

'*I think it's OK for the mediator to send A a draft letter to B for A to personalise and send. This seems to work well.*

'*Or, if the mediator is contacting B 'out of the blue', the letter needs to be carefully constructed. If A predicts that B is sure to refuse mediation, I write a kind of strategic letter to B which seems to work as they often phone immediately!*'

Lisa offers an example of a 'strategic letter' in the 1997 first edition of her book:

*Mr/Mrs...* does not think you will wish to take part in mediation, but I do hope you will consider speaking with me on your own to give your view of the situation and your children›s needs. Our conversation would be *confidential and I would not share any of it with Mr/Mrs .....without your permission. If you would be willing to speak on the phone ....*

'*I emphasise that it's important to check with party A that it's OK with them to tell B that A thinks B is unlikely to come to mediation. I found that A would typically say 'Yes, that's fine ... because he/she won't come....' B would however nearly always respond and A would be amazed when I said B was willing to mediate - sometimes it was A who wasn't keen and this called their bluff!'*

Lesley suggested the following wording:

*We have been given your details by [name] to offer you a mediation information and assessment appointment. We attach our literature for your information. Solicitors and the Courts encourage people to use mediation where possible. It is generally quicker, cheaper and often produces more effective agreements when couples need to sort out the practical aspects of separation.*

*We would be grateful if you would ring on receipt of this letter to arrange an appointment/and let us know your contact number.*

*We look forward to hearing from you.*

The sample below is an amalgamation of their advice and has worked well in practice with 100% response rate.

*We have been given your details by A to offer you a mediation information and assessment appointment. Solicitors and the Courts encourage people to use mediation where possible. It is generally quicker, cheaper and often produces more effective agreements when couples need to sort out the practical aspects of separation, and in your case, the possibility of A seeing his daughter, C.*

*I understand that you may be reluctant to engage in such a discussion; however, I would be grateful if you would ring on receipt of this letter so I can understand the situation from your perspective. My number is 07\*\*\*\*\*\*.*

*For more information about mediation, and in particular, Stratford Family Mediation please visit our website: www. stratfordfamilymediation.com/*

*I look forward to hearing from you.* [29]

---

29  If Mediation Vouchers are still available and you are qualified to apply for them, you could insert a sentence here, along these lines: 'The Ministry of Justice currently has a scheme which will pay £500 towards the cost of mediation cases which involve child arrangements, and I would be happy to apply for this grant on your behalf.'

# 21.
# A marketing strategy

*If you read nothing else in this section of the book, read this chapter!*

Strategies are good, but strategies too easily become industries in their own right.

There are marketing consultants out there – self-appointed 'gurus' – who can bore you to tears with theoretical outlines of marketing, using long words - sometimes to make themselves seem cleverer than they are! It means you can emerge with your own confidence dented, feeling a little less clever than you were when you entered the discussion. We're sure they don't mean to do this…

These chapters will definitely not do that!

We believe the best way to tackle the creation of a marketing strategy is to keep it simple.

So simple, in fact, that it can be boiled down to five words.

# The basics of marketing strategy

Put simply, in no particular order, these are:

- Who?
- What?
- Where?
- When?
- Why?

Let's pad that out a little:

- Who … are you trying to reach?
- What … will you say to them?
- Where … will you find them?
- When … will you say it?
- Why … are you doing this?

And to demonstrate these are in no particular order, you may look at that list and argue, for example, that the 'why' should go first.

So let's look in more detail at what we mean by these five W words.

# Who...
## are you trying to reach?

*This is about identifying the groups of people you need to reach in order to sell your 'product'.*

# Who do you want to 'tell your story' to?

What type of people are they? Well, adults, of course, but think about the age range, their interests (children and family, perhaps), the type of communities they live in, and so on.

# Where do they 'hang out'?

What physical places are they likely to visit and, therefore, perhaps see one of your leaflets or posters?

# What online spaces do they use?

Where do they hang out online? (eg Google, parents' forums, Facebook, Twitter.)

# Who else do they influence, and how?

If they influence others, does that make them more valuable to you? The concept of 'influencer' as a profession has become quite common in recent years, with the rise of YouTubers and Instagrammers.

But everyone influences other people in some way, with recommendations to friends and family members. You are bound to tell a potential client that your service is fantastic, but that message will be ten times more powerful if they hear it as an endorsement from someone they know and trust.

# What
## ... will you say to them?

*This is about defining your 'story' or 'message', and what you want people to do once they've heard it.*

## What is your 'story' or 'message'?

It can be helpful to think about marketing, press releases, campaigns, and other communications as 'storytelling'. The best campaigns develop and use narratives, to tell stories. People love stories!

If you met a potential client in a lift for 20 seconds, would you be able to be concise in explaining why they should use the service you offer? What story would you tell them in the lift? What would be your key message? We will return in more detail to this in a later chapter.

## What is the purpose of your message to them?

Are you trying to persuade them about something? Are you just providing them with information? Do you want them to take action immediately after they hear the story? The answer might well be 'yes' to all three, but unless you have asked yourself these questions, and know the answers, you will struggle to tell the story in the way that provokes the outcome you want.

## What ways do you envisage being known or represented?

As a champion of local families? A cheap option in divorce? As a trusted financial expert? A strong voice for family mediation in the local media? Again, it may be all of these, but don't overstretch yourself, and do be clear about your main strengths, so you can them market them appropriately.

## What is your story in 20 seconds?

Can you summarise the basics of your story in 20 seconds? Or on one side of A4? The ability to be concise is extremely important, and we will return to this shortly, with tips on how to get better at this vital skill.

## What narrative, or developing story, might there be?

Can you develop a narrative, so you tell a story over time? Think 'stories'. If your story has developing chapters, drip, drip, dripping your messages out to your audiences, then you are more likely to engage with people. No story book has just one section. Can you project ahead to what might come next in your story? This will be touched on a little more in the chapter about using the media.

# Where
# ... will you find them?

*This is all about the places that you need to go to reach those you want to reach*

## Where are the best spaces
## to tell your story?

We might be talking physical spaces here – the type of locations and facilities that people likely to need your service might hang out. Equally, and increasingly, we need to consider online spaces: what websites and social media channels do your potential clients use?

## Where are the geographical
## areas you need to target?

Do you serve just your local community? Does your service stretch beyond your town or city? What impact did the Covid-19 switch to video conference delivery have on your practice? Why wouldn't you now offer a Zoom service to people living 300 miles away?

## Where are the people you need to reach?
## What channels can you use to find them?

Whatever you do, don't answer this with 'all of them'. Anyone starting on a marketing exercise who decides to immediately have a presence on Facebook, Instagram, Twitter, LinkedIn, TickTock, Google Ads, Google MyBusiness, YouTube, Vimeo, news releases, opinion editorials, their own website, and other places will fail. They will massively overstretch themselves.

Do not use the argument that they need to be used 'because they're there.' Do one or two of the above well to begin with … rather than all of them badly! And think very carefully indeed which of the channels will be most productive for you in reaching potential clients.

When it comes to using the media, a potential way to reach clients 'free', through news releases, think very carefully which media are most likely to be interested in your story. It's obvious, but *The Times* is unlikely to run a front page story about you opening a new office in your town, whereas the family or business correspondent of your town's local free newspaper might. Again, start small - focus on two or three media outlets to begin with, and use the tips and ideas in the chapter about using the media.

## When
## … will you say it?

*This is about considering issues of timing, exactly when do you need to tell your story.*

## When? Now? Is it urgent?

Does it need to be out there immediately? If so, go for it. But do take a moment to distinguish the truly urgent from the "I want this off my 'to do' list so I can get on with other things". Timing is important in your business, as seasonal patterns show certain times of year are busier for services which help families in dispute.

## When does the next chapter of the story come?

Stories are so much more enjoyable and better-received when you can take your time over them. Think about over what period of time you want to tell your story. Do you have a series of chapters to tell? If so, do a simple timeline. On the back of an envelope is fine, as long as you keep the envelope for future reference!

## When the end is the beginning!

Reverse planning is important. By when do you need the story to be presented? Work backwards, starting from the successful conclusion of what you are planning (Facebook ad campaign, leaflet drop, local event or whatever) and plan a timeline.

*Example: The annual Family Mediation Week initiative takes place in mid-January every year. Don't wait until early January before you start planning what to do. Start in the autumn, so you have plenty of time, not just to do the preparation, but to refine the plans so they are brilliant, and not hurried. Look at the big picture too. Sketch out on a piece of paper (or an envelope, large!) the 12 months of the year ahead, and mark on a series of key 'events' or landmarks that you expect to influence your business. An obvious example is what's become known as 'Divorce Month' in January. School holidays might be among these too, as the long six-week one may test relationships and cause another rise in business for you.*

## Why
## ... are you doing this?

This is fundamental. And maybe it should the first in the list. Unless you are clear why you are trying to sell your services, you'll struggle to persuade anyone else.

## Why is it important to tell this story?

Maybe you believe your service can dramatically improve the lives of the people you want to reach. That it can reduce the massive stress faced by separating families. That your service can only survive and thrive if you get enough 'bums on seats' at your service. Again, all these might be true, but be very clear in your own mind what, exactly, you are trying to achieve, and why you want people to hear your message.

## Why your business plan is key

Is your goal to increase numbers of people coming through the doors to a MIAM? Is a more important factor for you ensuring a better conversion rate from MIAM to mediation? What specialisms does your service offer? These and other questions will be driven by your own business plan, and your marketing strategy needs to be aligned with it.

## Why business-to-business marketing is important

If your service is just starting, you will probably want to begin to build an identity in the community you want to serve, and boosting client numbers will be key to this. If you're well-established it might be more about a wish to widen your community – perhaps serving a larger geographical area, or increasing the types of services you offer.  But is it just about potential clients? You will probably want to focus on developing a reputation amongst fellow professionals, in business-to-business (B2B) circles so that, for example, local solicitors or the family court know you're there, and might refer potential clients to you.

# 22.
# Identifying your target audiences & working out how best to reach them

## What are your target audiences?

If you are going to reach them, you need to know.

- Who they are, what type of people?

What sort of life situations are your potential clients currently in? Remember that people experiencing life crises are often experiencing a crisis in areas of their lives not limited only to 'family' ones.

- Where you can find them, where do they hang out?

These people will be hanging out in a variety of places, some physical 'actual' places, and other virtual, online spaces.

Identifying and making lists of where these people might be hanging out, in your local area and perhaps beyond, is an important task to do at the outset.

In fact, it's two lists: one of the physical places they may go, and the other is the online spaces they visit.

We are going to consider online spaces in detail in a later chapter, so for now it may be best to focus mainly on *actual locations* that people you are likely to deem potential clients might visit. Sometimes they'll make these visits as a positive matter of choice, and sometimes of necessity.

**Whatever you want to sell, whatever message you want to get across, you'll find it far easier to go where they currently are, than hoping or expecting they'll come to you. Yes, that's obvious when you think about it, but never forget it when you're marketing anything.**

You need to go and find them, and this has major implications for everything you do in marketing terms.

*TASK: Where did they come from?*

*Thinking about clients that have come to you in the past month or so, take one minute to write down where you found them. Or, perhaps more accurately, where they found you, and how they arrived at your 'door'.*

*Now turn the page to see some examples of places that other mediators who've done this task have listed as sources of referrals.*

*By the way, if you don't ask your clients how they found out about you, you are missing a major trick. If you don't do this, you won't be able to understand your successful referrals. This is important for two reasons: you will then be better-placed to multiply referrals from those places; and you will be able to see which of the potential referral sources you would expect to be getting clients aren't in fact providing leads, and take steps to address this.*

**Where do you find your clients?**

- Word of mouth
- Citizens Advice and other advice networks
- NHS
- Child Contact Centres
- Parents' groups
- Solicitors
- LinkedIn
- Social services
- Local community organisations
- GPs
- Police
- Schools
- Web searches
- Job Centres
- Faith groups
- Facebook
- Community centres
- Children / family centres
- Family court
- Newspapers and other media
- Paid adverts
- Leaflets

- Public transport
- Family Mediation Council website search
- Supermarket notice boards
- HR departments
- High Street / coffee shops

So these are 'places' you can go to find client referrals. Don't go to every one of them on Day 1 of your marketing plan, but pick two to five of them to really focus on to begin with.

One noticeable thing about the list above is that most of these are 'physical' places. Covid-19 induced lockdowns really threw into sharp focus a major challenge facing those who rely on these actual places to which access was not available. Online spaces are just as, if not more, important for your marketing activities. That's why we've dedicated a whole chapter to this later on.

The list above can be grouped roughly into two. The first group is made up of the places where you reach a potential client *directly* (eg Facebook campaign, notice on supermarket notice board). The second is made up of those where you are reliant on a *'third party'* to pass your information on or to recommend you (eg CAB, local solicitor).

Bearing this in mind, now, go back to the full list and think about which are 'Direct-to-client', and which are 'via third party referrers.'

There may be some grey areas here: for example, if you want leaflets available in a community centre, you'll have to ask the centre manager's permission, and don't get too hung up on this exercise. You don't *have* to write the two lists, but the exercise is useful because when you nail down your marketing plan, this distinction should be an important part of your thinking.

## RECAP: You reach your potential clients by going where they are

The precise nature of the services you offer, and the specialisms you provide, will shape where to go to find them.

- Locations they visit
- Media they read
- Online spaces they use

The importance of finding out from where you currently get client referrals is again underlined here, because understanding where the gaps in current referrals are will help direct you to some places you're missing out on.

For example, if in the last three months you've had no referrals from the local Citizens Advice, maybe you need to look at refreshing your relationship-building with the staff there. In a later chapter we focus a little more on these 'third party referrers'.

## The changing landscape of marketing family mediation

Covid-19 changed the landscape of marketing for a whole range of products and services, including family mediation.

The way that people were expected to realign their working and family lives during the lockdowns undoubtedly changed the habits and expectations of millions of people.

Let's use the Covid-19 experience to trigger important marketing considerations such as: How important is your geographical reach right now? How limited should your marketing be to your local area? Of course this has implications for 'going where they go'.

This is not to say that local targeting has had its day. Far from it, as humans like local contact and can be loyal to their community, valuing trust, locality and the ability to drop-in to see a professional provider face-to-face will still be important in future, perhaps even more than before the pandemic. Sadly, we don't have a crystal ball.

## House conveyancing

Let's drift away from family mediation marketing for a moment. If you've ever bought or sold a house, you'll be familiar with the fact that you need a conveyancing solicitor to sort the legal aspects of your deal.

The development of the internet changed the landscape of conveyancing marketing, opening up the market for house buyers and sellers well beyond their local area. Yes, estate agents will still have arrangements with local solicitor firms whereby they recommend their house-buying client should use Laurel, Hardy and Costello & Partners.

But the shrewd house-buyer understands they can visit The Homeowners Alliance website and get a price comparison which can save hundreds of pounds on the estate agent-recommendation, employing a conveyancer based hundreds of miles away.

What's the relevance of this? Well, the mushrooming of video conference mediation during the pandemic just might represent a family mediation game-changer similar to conveyancing comparison websites. We are not saying it will, but that it might. What will be the shape of family mediation in ten years from the date you're reading this? Thinking through this type of question can give you an important marketing edge. Some people call it 'horizon-scanning'. But it's really just a matter of thinking ahead so you can be in front of a changing game, not behind it.

# 23.
# Getting your message right

## Defining your top-line message by using the Elevator Test

You may well have heard of, or tried, the elevator test. Many people are familiar with it. It's worth a fresh look in the context of your marketing plans as you look to develop a top-line message.

Imagine you get into an elevator on the ground floor of a tall building. You're going to Level 8 so that's the button you press. The elevator stops at Level 2 and someone gets in that you recognise, and you want to seize the moment to introduce yourself to them, so they know who you are and what value you might bring them. They press the button for Level 7.

This means you have about 20 seconds to introduce yourself and say what you need to say. 20 seconds isn't long! Being concise is vital.

Now, if you imagine the person getting in this 'elevator' is a potential client, what would you say to them face-to-face? You've still only got 20 seconds to leave them with a memorable impression of your service offer.

*TASK. Say to yourself what you would envisage saying to a potential client about your service and why it could be of great value to them.*

*Get a stopwatch and repeat the above task. The aim is to create two or three concise sentences that sum up the value and benefit of your service to this imaginary potential client in this imagining elevator – where the sentences, when spoken, last no more than 20 seconds. And beware, don't fall into the trap of just saying five or six sentences very, very quickly!*

*This can be tough. There are all sorts of reasons why your service will bring value and benefit to potential clients. The trick is distilling these into a set of short sentences or phrases that best convey your services' qualities that can be used as your top-line messaging to appear in your marketing activities and materials.*

*Take your time and practice, practice, practice. Write down, or voice-record, all the drafts you come up with.*

In the above task, you may have found that just as you get to a point where you think you've nailed the best words, you then realise you've missed out one of your service's star qualities. Don't worry!

If you've come across the elevator test in a personal capacity, it will usually be to help you to prepare to introduce yourself to others, perhaps at a conference or meeting.

The purpose of this marketing exercise is to get you to really drill down into what star qualities your service can offer. To get as much meaning in to the time available.

You may believe that potential clients will read every word of an advertisement you publish in the local paper, or that they will pore over your Facebook ad. They won't. They're busy people, like you.

You've got to grab their attention and make it abundantly clear within a few words, what value you can bring to their lives.

If you found this hard, please don't feel defeated or deflated. Or both. It IS hard. But it's a vital part of your story. Think of the blurbs on the back of a novel by an unknown author that you might pick up in a busy train station. They will probably determine whether you buy the book or not.

The process of thinking through your service's qualities, and articulating them in what initially feels like a messy way, is a key part of getting your top-line message across.

Why 20 seconds? Yes, it's a red herring and of course it doesn't HAVE to be that length. It might be 30, or 40, or even just 15. The important thing is getting used to being disciplined and concise when creating your message.

Of course, if you are planning to write a leaflet, or some introductory words for your website, you will have space to write more than what you could say in 20 seconds. But that leaflet and web page will need some sort of title, and introductory sentences, and these need to be concise to draw the reader in to go further.

## How can you further improve your messaging?

*There are a number of things to consider when you undertake the vital tasks relating to defining and perfecting your message:*

## How do you want to be perceived?

Here are some examples of the strengths that you might believe apply to your service, and that you may therefore wish to include in your message:

- Champion of local families
- Supportive presence
- Friendly to deal with
- Competent over money & parenting agreements
- Impartial in negotiations

You will be able to think of other examples to add to this list. Think carefully about which of these are your greatest assets when trying to secure business. You might think you meet all of the bullet points above. Yes, you might, but don't overstretch or over-elaborate. Choose the most powerful asset or assets you have, and try to incorporate them into your top-line message.

## Developing your message on from the top-line 20 seconds

Do read on. You are unlikely, at this stage, to have perfected that 20 second top-line pitch. However, that top-line ends up, you will need more 'message' to add to your story if you are going to convert potential clients into actual clients.

## The relative ease of selling trainers, handbags and kitchen knives

If you were selling trainers, or handbags, or kitchen knives, you would of course be selling a product whose function everyone understands. We all know what a running shoe or a handbag does. We know what we expect from a kitchen knife. Finely sliced onions. If only marketing your service was as straightforward.

## The relative challenges of selling family mediation

Family mediation is different, and not just because many people do not understand what is entails. It is probably fair to say that ultimately you are actually trying to sell a way of life for a family's future, rather than a product or service.

If you're a kitchen knife merchant, you will probably emphasise the outcome the client would reap – those finely sliced onions and perfect carrots. For ordinary members of the public, the outcomes of family mediation are far harder to envisage. But it is vital that you articulate these: a brighter way ahead for the whole family, for example.

You want clients to project to the future and, whilst it seems glib to say so, this applies equally to kitchen knives and mediation: sliced onions or amicable parenting arrangements where both parents remain close to the kids!

## Outcomes and processes

There is a difficult balance to achieve here. You do need to help potential clients understand something about the *processes* of mediation, and what steps they will need to be involved in when they commit to undertaking the mediation journey. But perhaps more important to the client in the early stage is understanding where the mediation journey will end: what the outcomes for the family could be.

But even before you get to that stage, add to the mix the fact that in their minds they will be balancing the pros and cons of family mediation as compared with commissioning a solicitor to go into battle on their behalf. You need to help them understand the benefits of mediation compared with the 'lawyer route'. If they don't understand those benefits, there's no real chance they'll end up as a client of yours.

The MIAM now being compulsory is of course helpful in this regard, as is widespread messaging about the value and benefits of mediation. But be prepared to do your bit in selling the *very concept* of mediation to every potential client. After all, if they've initially come to you thinking they can simply tick off the MIAM before going into battle, you can save them from all that stress and expense if you articulate the benefits to them of undertaking mediation.

Once clients have been convinced they need to try mediation – regardless of whether they initially want to tick a MIAM box or because they are convinced that mediation could work for them – you now need to articulate you own unique selling points. There will probably be other family mediators working in the local area and you need to articulate how and why your service is their best option.

To do this, think about your own service's unique selling points. This might include your

- distinctive way of working
- people
- track record
- years' experience
- specialist services (child-inclusive, shuttle, video conference, etc.)
- prices
- flexibility
- speed of turnaround from initial enquiry to appointment
- location and accessibility

## Three vital stages to developing your story

It might be helpful to include all of the following stages as you develop your message story.

# 1. The future

Why mediation? Focus on the long-term outcome: projecting a brighter future

# 2. The short-term

Why mediation? Focus on the short-term benefits: cheaper, quicker, less stressful

# 3. My next step

Why us? Your unique selling points

This is not a prescription for the order in which you make your points in your story, or how to write a leaflet, ad or website introduction. It is simply to say that unless you include these three elements you could miss a vital stage in the potential client's thinking.

## Principles of your messaging

- Start from where clients are, not where you want them to be.

Just as you are urged elsewhere in this book to go to the *places* where potential clients visit and hang out, not where you'd like them to visit, you should also apply this principle to the client's prior knowledge and current head space.

- Think how you demonstrate that you can take them to where they want to get to.

Your job is to 'move them on' to the next stage in their lives, and you need to help them see that your service can help them achieve this movement to the more positive stage.

- Listen carefully to client feedback.

It can feel time-consuming and distracting to log details of the strengths and weaknesses clients have identified in your service. But if you are to improve the service you offer you must do this, and take action to address weaknesses. By the way, positive client comments can be used as endorsements for your advertising material, so don't be frightened to ask clients for permission to use them in this way.

And remember what has been said before about the value of logging and analysing the source of the client: how they found you, and what attracted them to you. Try to avoid this simply being a multi-choice tick-box (Facebook, Google search, etc.). Dig deeper if you can; exactly what about your service was attractive to them: cost, location, accessibility, specialist services such as child-inclusive mediation, and so on. This qualitative analysis is far better at helping you understand your strengths and, therefore, will help you develop and refine your message.

There is an example of one mediator who believed that her 12 years' experience as a mediator was a great selling-point for her. She trumpeted this as in her marketing efforts as a key reason clients should use her services. Digging deeper into the reasons people used the service, however, it became clear they didn't really care about this. It was her High Street location that sold the service for itself.

- Use simple language

Beware of jargon. Language can be daunting or confusing. Never assume they know what 'MIAM', 'shuttle' or even 'Client 2 or Client B' means to you. These terms may mean nothing to them.

- Take time to distil it right down: no more than three bullets.

Look at this fantastic quote, from Mark Twain, writer, lecturer and publisher:

*"I apologise for such a long letter - I didn't have time to write a short one."*

It takes time to be concise.

*TASK: Taking the principle of the Elevator Test, can you write down your main message in no more than three sentences or three bullet points?*

- Script conversations to ensure conversion.

When talking to potential clients on the phone, it's worth writing a 'script' for those conversations to ensure you convert them to MIAM or to full mediation. All your carefully crafted messaging might fall to pieces if you don't make the most of what they have already read about you.

You need to ensure that what you say to them on the phone, or when they visit your office, matches how you have portrayed your service elsewhere. The 'script' shouldn't oversell yourself, but ensure you tell them what you want them to know in order to help get them on your side.

And by the way, 'script' doesn't mean you read something out to them in a wooden manner resembling a six year-old's single line in a nativity play! It might just be a bullet point list of three or four key things you need to cover in that conversation.

- Consistency across channels.

Your key messaging needs to be used everywhere your service has a public presence. If a client reads about you on your website, but then in your Facebook page profile a whole different set of words is used, proclaiming different service strengths, then the client will wonder if it's the same organisation. They might think: 'Have I come to the right place?' They should be in doubt.

Coca-Cola has one logo that it uses worldwide. So do most organisations, global, national or local. You should have one set of key messages that you use everywhere to help ensure you are recognised in whatever channel or publication you are seen[30].

---

30 As mentioned in the previous chapter on Pictures, using the same profile photo on your website and social media aids recognition and consistency.

# 24.
# Understanding online audiences

## Social Media Channels Explained:

Facebook        I like chocolate muffins

Twitter         I'm eating a #chocolatemuffin

Pinterest       Here's a chocolate muffin recipe

Instagram       Here's a picture of my chocolate muffin

LinkedIn        My skills include chocolate muffin eating

Google+         I'm a Google employee who eats chocolate muffins[31]

---

31  After Foxxglove Media

The challenge writing a book which aims to help readers understand online audience is, of course, that online channels are always evolving. We could go into great depth about the merits of Twitter, say, or Instagram. But who knows where those channels will be in three, five, ten years' time? And who knows what new channels will have come along.

You don't need to jump on the next available bandwagon, though. We've lost count of the number of times clients have wanted to set up an Instagram account, or a Snapchat. They'd heard about these channels, maybe even use them in their personal life. So they've got to have them for work, right? Well, no, actually.

Take Instagram, for example. It is all about pictures. And not just that, but it's all about pictures that will be very small when viewed, because people use Instagram on mobiles.

If your business does not generate great pictures, often and regularly, then you'll do well to forget having an Instagram account. Mediation clients very rarely want to be photographed and used for your marketing purposes. They want to 'move on' in their lives. Even if you generate some good infographics, with great data represented pictorially, remember that these could be hard to see on a mobile screen.

So rather than leaping on the next big thing, always stick true to the principles that have been laid out in this book so far.

Please read on as we give you some information about some of the main online channels that you may wish to use.

But primarily please note carefully the most important message we have for you in this chapter: Identify your audiences, how to reach them, and get your message right. The channels used to deliver these will change over time. You only need to think back 10 or 20 years from the day you're reading this book. Newspapers. Remember them? The fact their importance waned does not in any way diminish the importance of the principles being outlined in these chapters, which would have been identical had this book been written in 1995 when actual newspapers that people went out and bought were the only game in town. Times change, principles shouldn't.

Everything is online. Some therefore think that 'online is everything'. It isn't. But ignore it at your peril, and get up to speed on some of the channels available, and what they might offer you.

**Need-to-know: Join us on a whistle-stop tour of some online tools and channels**

Please note that it is assumed you have a very basic understanding of the tools and channels listed below. We are not going to explain in detail the mechanics of exactly what Twitter actually is, for example. We think and assume you'll have heard of these channels and that you are reading this because you want to know more about how best to use them in your communications and marketing. (Also see Chapter 14 Track Website Behaviour and Goals.)

# Google Ads

If you do a Google web search, you will see on screen a long list of websites that Google is recommending match your search. Often at the top of the screen you will see one or two of these links that say 'ad' next to them. Guess what? Yes, these listings are ads. Companies have paid Google for these, on the basis that they will appear at the top of your search results page and therefore you're most likely to click on them.

The advertiser only pays any money to Google if the link in the listing is clicked on, taking the user to the advertiser's website. The advertiser uses the Google Ads dashboard (which is basically another website) and there it defines a series of key words and phrases that it wants to target.

So a central heating engineer might identify key words such as, say, 'leaking radiator in Brighton' or 'central heating not working' as being the type of Google search for which it wishes to be listed at the top of the search results page.

The advertiser bids for the right to have the ad shown, and the competition for each key word determines how much it will cost them each time the link is clicked[32].

The advertiser sets a budget, so that if the ad proves extremely popular, they won't get stung for more money than they can afford.

---

32 Catherine tried Google Ads and found that popular key words could cost more than £8 per click.

It's well worth investigating Google Ads for your business, because amongst other things you can decide:

- keywords you bid for
- location/s to target, so if you only want clients from your town or city that's all you'l get
- which page you send users to when they click.

Like Google Analytics, there is a huge amount of data available to you so you can carefully analyse how effective your Ads are. Incidentally, non-profit organisations get free entitlements.

## Google My Business

This is a facility available on Google Maps, so that users can type in a phrase, rather than an address or location. You may be thirsty and so type in 'bars'. Google Maps will then show you local bars on the map. The same applies to all sorts of businesses, including yours.

It could be worth getting a listing on this free facility, especially if your focus is on your local geographical area. It can help people locate your business, drive traffic to your website, and find your contact details. Like a number of other channels, though, if you use it, make sure you keep it up to date. During the Covid-19 pandemic, so many businesses appeared as 'open', when they were closed, but had forgotten to update their business hours.

And be aware that people can leave reviews of your business on this facility, so keep an eye on those too.

# Family Mediation Council website

Never forget that the FMC website lists, as part of a search, all accredited mediators, with the space for a picture, contact details and services offered. Keep it up to date. Just as many businesses appeared with outdated information on Google My Business during the pandemic, so did many family mediators, who hadn't thought to update their entry to show they had begun offering video conference mediation.

# Twitter

It's a cocktail party, open to the whole world!

- Have a profile that describes you the way you'd want to be introduced at that party.

Use a scheduling tool such as tweetdeck.com

- Schedule posts to suit you, so that you ensure you can be issuing tweets even when you're away from your device!

Use hashtags

- They start with this # (which is called a hashtag!)
- Search them, and 'jump' on them when it's appropriate. Clients will not be watching your Twitter timeline, believe us! But they may well search #mediation or #familymediation to find providers. The same applies to those organisations

and individuals that you may want to engage with in a business-to-business manner, for example possible referrers to you, from CABs or other advice networks.

- Be topical and aware of current 'trends' and events.

Follow your referrers and potential referrers.

- Use @mentions to engage with them.
- Retweet them.
- 'Like' their tweets.
- Direct Message ('DM') them.
- 'Who to follow' (suggestions by Twitter) can sometimes help.
- Keep an eye on your competitors' activity.

Use images (and video)

- Suitable free stock pictures are available if you look on the internet. (See Chapter 15)

Study your Analytics

- This is a standard part of your Twitter menu. Look carefully at the number of views your tweets get at different times of the day, what hashtags you used led to increased views, and what style or type of content of tweet got most 'likes' and retweets.

Include links to your website

- And / or to items of interest / relevance elsewhere.

- Use short links to save space. You can use the free site bit.ly which generates these for you.

Don't be afraid to repeat tweets: timelines move quickly.

Watch your notifications and DMs, and respond.

Remember its potential to help you reach the third party referrers you need to engage, but ... keep it in context. Bear in mind its effectiveness in reaching your targets, compared with other methods. In fact, for your clients it's unlikely to be hugely significant.

And remember your Twitter audience is a largely 'cold' one. Don't expect clients to 'follow' you. Mediation is a crisis purchase, and they won't want their friends to see they're following an organisation like yours. After they've finished using your service they will want to move on.

## Facebook Page

Note carefully the reference above to Facebook Page, not profile. Your business presence on Facebook, should you choose to have one, should be separate from your own personal profile, although you may choose to make your personal profile an administrator ('page admin') of the business page. This means you log into your Facebook personal profile to then be able to edit the business page.

Personal profiles are for the 'closed house party' that is Facebook, and you need approval to get in - you need to be 'friends' with other personal profiles. But a Facebook business page is visible to anyone when they are using their personal profile. So have a profile that describes you the way you'd want to be known.

Consider paid advertising.

- You can target who sees your ad by: gender, age, interests and location. And you can decide how much to spend. Facebook ads or 'boosted posts' can be quite a low-cost way to reach an audience. You set your budget over a period of days. By narrowing down the audience that will see your ad, you will save money too.

    Use the Insights & Ad Center features to understand your audience's behaviours

- This is essential if you are paying for ads as you will be able to see a wealth of data about numbers of people seeing your ad, clicking on any link within it, and so on.

Schedule posts

- Within the 'Publishing Tools' option of your page so that, as with Twitter above you can schedule posts and then walk away for days at a time.

    'Like' the pages of your referrers and potential referrers. Use mentions of their pages in posts to engage with them. Share their posts to your followers. And keep an eye on your competitors.

Use images (and video)

- Make your own
  Try to say something interesting and engaging.

Include links to your website.

Watch your notifications, comments on your post, and inbox – and respond where necessary.

Keep it in context at all times. Like Twitter, Facebook can be a useful tool, but it's not the only one available to you.

## Instagram

As we've already pointed out, Instagram is all about pictures that can be seen on mobile phones. If your service generates loads of great pictures, then it might be right for you to go for it. However, don't drown in the enthusiasm of setting up an Instagram account, posting three pictures in three days, and then forgetting it's there. That could actually damage your business reputation since any potential client finding you there may see the page is dormant and assume you've stopped trading.

## YouTube

The same comments about Instagram apply to YouTube, yet replacing 'pictures' with videos. At the time of writing, YouTube is the internet's second-largest search engine. It's a hub of useful content if you need, for example, to know how to fix a broken toilet flush, or perform other DIY tasks. Unless you have a decent budget to make good quality videos, however, it's unlikely to be a brilliant channel for your service.

## LinkedIn

Having a presence on LinkedIn can be a good way of making business links with other professionals and, therefore, potential referrers. And speaking of referrers, let's conclude this whistle-stop tour, and move to our next chapter.

# 25.
# Finding and nurturing 'third party' referrers

We've talked earlier in these chapters about the difference between the way you communicate with potential clients either through 'direct-to-client' channels, or via 'third party referrers.'

Most of the content so far has focused on direct-to-client channels. In this and the following chapter we will focus on those where you are to some extent reliant on others: what we call 'third parties', and the media.

When we talk about third party referrers here, we are looking primarily at what you might call 'business-to-business' communications. Call it indirect marketing if you like. Call it whatever you want, in fact, but read this short chapter and you'll understand what it is. Then maybe give it your own name!

# Know who they are and where to find them

Spend some time making lists of the third party referrers that matter to you. Be exhaustive. List them all. Go back to the chapter where we considered 'Where do you find your clients?' for suggested types of organisations.

Get up-to-date names and contact details of key people working there. You might want to refine your list and prioritise, because this can be a time-consuming task. Contacting advice networks, for example, can be frustrating because a) the lines are often busy, b) staff and volunteers there may only work on certain days, and c) turnover might be quite high, so your hard-won contact list needs refreshing every few months.

But unless you know how to contact them, how are you going to send them your latest leaflets, invite them to events or conference calls, or inform them of the new services you might be offering?

# Build relationships

Call or email them occasionally. Schedule a reminder in your calendar every three months to ring to check they've got enough of your leaflets.

If it's practical to do so, drop in to say hello when you give them a new batch of leaflets. Face to face contact resonates much, much more than a 'cold' email. And invite them to a drop-in event[33] and try to attend theirs, or at least take an interest. Maybe you could even jointly host drop-in events.

And don't forget to follow them on social media channels, perhaps 'liking' or sharing their posts occasionally. It feels old-hat to say 'send a Christmas card', but don't let them forget you.

---

33 For example, Beverley Sayers held a cheese and wine evening for solicitors

# 26.
# Using the media

## Symbiosis

The majority of these chapters are aimed at helping you craft and deliver material that you use to reach your potential clients directly. That's to say, they will read your Facebook post, your leaflet, your website, exactly as you wrote it. It reaches them in undiluted form.

Getting your messages across via the media (newspapers, community newsletters and online news channels) is slightly different, because the media is a go-between. Unless you pay for an advert, you are reliant on a journalist to publish your story. And that means their interpretation of the story you give them.

To many people, journalists and news publications are a bit scary because it's considered they hold all the cards. They publish what they want to publish, after all.

Even though you may feel this way, be clear with yourself that the relationship you have with a journalist is in fact a symbiotic one. You both rely on each other. Taking this view can transform the way you view the media and your prospects of getting stories published.

Symbiotic? How? Well, yes, you need *them* to publish your story, but newspaper offices are very often understaffed, and they have pages or airspace to fill. And it's relentless: no sooner has the editor of a local printed news publication submitted the week's content to print than they need to start generating content for the following week.

Local radio news editors are under continual daily pressure to come up with stories, guests, and interesting angles on issues that are of interest to their audience.

So, you supplying them with a good story is really helpful to them. Think of issuing a news release as a good deed for the day - a random act of kindness, perhaps!

There are people who say journalists are lazy. Others say they are extremely busy people. Whichever view is correct, it is true that if you write your news release as you would an article in a newspaper, it could well get copied and pasted in full in the paper or on the website.

## Some initial steps

First, let's walk through a series of steps that you'd do well to consider before you embark on your efforts to use the media.

1. Define *why* you want media coverage. Be clear about your objectives. You may want to generally raise your profile in the communities you serve, or have identified that you're not getting many clients from a certain town and so want to focus media efforts there to boost business. Or you may be looking for additional clout in business-to-business circles.

2. Define *where* you want media coverage. You will have considered in your business plan the 'reach' of your service, and the pool of people you want to target. Geography is an important part of this. You may have decided to only seek clients from the city or town you're based in, or to have a specific set of postcodes that you serve. This decision will inform your media plan.

3. Define what it is that makes your organisation of interest to 'ordinary' local people. The media needs to serve its specific audience, so needs stories that are genuinely interesting to them. As we said earlier, you are a champion of local families, a cheap option in divorce, a trusted financial expert, a strong voice on divorce. And remember that the media love conflict in all forms, because conflict generates great stories. And as a family mediator you're at the heart of conflict!

4. Define how you want to be represented. This might seem the same as the point above, but this is specifically about deploying the 'power' you hold, so you can ensure that your stories are representing you accurately. Perhaps you want to be seen as a friendly and supportive local facility, a vocal critic of family law policy, a competent expert in finance, or an experienced wise old head with a strong track record.

# Do your background research

Spend some time getting up-to-date contact details, email and phone, for all the relevant news outlets in the area you want to serve. Be aware that many tend to have a high staff turnover, so don't be tempted to rely on an old contact list from three or four years ago. If this media stuff is worth doing, it's worth doing well.

Make a new list of online, 'mass' newspapers, and free community newspapers. The latter have become increasingly important and trusted by audiences. Fewer people buy newspapers, but the ones that come through your door or that you pick up in the supermarket or petrol station, that are truly local, are hugely important to readers and therefore to you too.

Talk to others to ensure you've covered all the outlets. A colleague or friend who lives in a different part of the city may tell you about a local paper they receive that you'd never heard of.

And remember that some publications have different journalists for different issues. So you might want to focus on, say, the business specialist, the family correspondent, and so on.

How do you get the contact details? Well, desktop research is a good start, but so is the telephone. Calling a newspaper office on the basis that, say, you're checking the right email address to send a news release to is a great way to introduce yourself and your service. It may lead to a conversation with a journalist in which you plant the seed of the story. Don't forget, though, that they are busy, so don't expect it in this initial call.

## Okay, what shall we write about?

**Here are some principles to bear in mind when considering what makes a good story:**

- Make it human

Your story is only going to be of interest to the extent that it affects or touches upon the lives and livelihoods of people reading it, and their families.

- Make it relevant

Ask yourself "How does this or might this affect readers' lives?" What's in it for them? If you think a reader will just say 'so what?' then rethink whether to bother writing the story.

- Make it topical

Doing a story that is connected to a current or recent event or issue that's playing out – local to you or national – can make it stronger and more likely to be picked up by journalists[34].

- Make it local

---

34  For example, the recent MOJ £500 Mediation Voucher Scheme

Readers are only interested in what's happening in their community. National or regional statistics might be a good starting point, but the smaller the geographical focus the better. Try to bring it as close to street or community level as you can.

**Here are some 'pegs' to hang your story on**

- Firsts – in your city, your region, your country
- Special one-off activities and events
- Openings of offices or new services
- Becoming the best, or one of the best
- Key milestones and anniversaries
- Changes, refurbishments, re-openings
- Celebrity visits
- Innovative ideas
- New staff appointments
- Links with other organisations in your community
- Jumping aboard current / recent events
- Letters to the editor
- Pitching an 'expert voice' article
- Client case studies

**You've got your idea… how do you write a news release?**

The best way to demonstrate this is with a model news release.

## Short headline covering the key facts

*Your first paragraph is the most important. Start with a simple statement, and then try to get the essence of your message across.*

*Some busy journalists won't read past your first paragraph. So make it count.*

*Use your second paragraph to expand on the points raised in the first. If the journalist gets this far, they're taking an interest. So you can afford to go into a bit more detail. But not too much. It's probably best to use 'notes for editors' at the foot of the release for more in-depth stuff.*

*Avoid using exclamation marks! AND DON'T USE CAPITAL LETTERS FOR EFFECT. Try and keep the whole news release less than a page of A4: the shorter the better.*

*"At this point include a helpful quote", said communications consultant Richard Wyatt. "Make every word count. Don't repeat things you've said in your opening paragraph, but do take the opportunity to build on them. The more interesting your quote, the more likely it will be used.*

*"If you follow these simple guidelines, you have a much better chance of getting journalists to take note of your news release," he added.*

*At this point, if there remain any points you still want to convey, do so. But try to keep it short. If by this stage you haven't yet been able to highlight your key message then try to do it now. If you already have done so, then do it again, using different words.*

## Photograph or filming opportunity

*If you are offering a photo / filming opportunity, or even if you are open to the journalist trying to arrange one, do mention this. For pre-arranged ones, such as events, give clear details of location (with directions and postcode) date, time and what will be happening. It's also worth including a reference to the media opportunity in the news release headline e.g. 'News and photograph opportunity from xxxxx:* **Short snappy headline covering the key facts***'*

*But DO consider attaching a photo you've already taken. Make sure at this point you refer to the photo and say exactly what it shows, repeating full names and role titles.*

## Notes for editor:

*1. You can use this space to communicate a few more details and essential background information.*

*2. You might also include links to web pages which contain key info, removing the need to go into depth in your short news release. Interested journalists will click through, so be sure to check your link (and what follows from it) in case it might draw attention to something else.*

## For more information contact

*Name, title, phone number (one that is going to be answered by you) and email.*

# What do you do with the news release?

- Paste it into the body of an email. Don't' send it as an attachment because many email programs block attachments. And even if it gets through, many journalists won't do the extra click needed to open it
- If it's going to a few different journalists, send it to yourself and blind copy them. Better still send individual emails, and top and tail it with a single line 'Hope this is of interest. Let me know if you'd like more information'-type
- A few minutes later, call the journalists to check they received it. This can open up a conversation where you can perhaps tell them a bit more about the story, or just paraphrase it for them. It could be the beginning of a beautiful relationship!

# What if they follow up with a phone call?

- Hurrah! They're interested: it's a chance to shine!
- Find out why they are interested in the story and what sort of comment they want from you (we assume that's why they're calling you).
- Try to buy time and get a deadline for your comments.
- Write some words down and email the comment to the journalist.
- Or call them back with a scripted comment.

By the way, if they don't call it could mean they don't need to, because your news release covered everything they needed to publish the story.

## Some more tips...

- Identify media opportunities in good time: plan ahead with a media timeline so you pace your media effort over several weeks and months.
- A picture speaks a thousand words. Sending a good picture with your news release can increase the chance of it being covered. But not just two people gormlessly looking at a camera. Try to get them 'doing' something in the picture.
- Be retrospective if you have to. If your event or landmark has already passed, don't give up on it. You could write a retrospective news release in the past tense.
- Accept there are no guarantees that you will receive coverage.
- Evaluate. Reflect on the news releases you have issued and which got picked up. And which ones didn't. Try to understand why this might be. And don't be frightened to call the journalist to ask how best you can help them by improving the stories you give them.
- Nurture your relationships. Send them a Christmas card!

# A word about client case studies ...

These are gold dust. If you are able to get a satisfied client to go on the record to talk about how good mediation and your service was, it really brings the story to life. If a journalist shows interest in your story, they may ask if you've got a case study person they can interview.

Think about when you watch a TV news feature about, say, a government change to the benefit system. It will usually begin with film of a real person affected by the change, talking about the impact. The politician responsible might get a 10 second clip somewhere later on in the feature, but it's the real-life human element that is the focus, because that's what the audience will be most interested in.

You are bound to say how good your service is, aren't you? But a real person saying this has tons more impact. Don't take this personally, but listeners and viewers trust 'real' people more than you!

The mediator is best placed to secure the case study. By asking. That's often the most difficult part. Assuming they will say 'no'. And it's true that most people will say 'no', because they just want to move on with their lives. But that one in ten could prove to be a powerful advocate for your service.

And when someone agrees, you might try to be helpful by indicating the type of things they may want to say when they're being interviewed.

# 27.
# Planning your next steps in 20 minutes

We're near the end. It's tempting to now close the book. Don't!

Whatever you do after reading these chapters, don't just put the book on the shelf without spending at least 20 minutes writing a quick action plan.

Yes, just 20 minutes.

A little more if you like, but the very process of writing down some immediate next steps will, whether you realise it or not, unconsciously commit you to action.

And it's important to do this right away. Yes, now! We've all been on training courses which we found useful. Then forgotten all the useful stuff when we got back to the office and got swamped with emails, calls and all the rest of it.

At the beginning we talked about these chapters being for people who prefer simplicity and common sense.

Simplicity it is. Spend 20 minutes completing the grid below.
This gives you a two-month starter plan. Keep the completed
plan on your desk or wall so it's in your mind and, of course,
use the pages that precede this one to guide you.

And in case this 20-minute task still feels too hard, beneath the
grid you'll find some examples of things you might include in
the Objective column. You're very welcome!

| Objective | To achieve this, my next step is... | Task/s in December | Task/s in January | How I will evaluate success |
|---|---|---|---|---|
|  |  |  |  |  |
|  |  |  |  |  |
|  |  |  |  |  |
|  |  |  |  |  |

Your objectives might include:

- Strengthen relationships with referrer A, B and C in your area
- Investigate Google Analytics: know how people use your site
- Set up a Facebook page
- Improve your FMC listing / Google My Business
- Investigate Google Ads
- Study hashtags on Twitter
- Review the content on your website
- Refine your core messages (no more than three short bullets)
- Design / print a simple flyer and go to the supermarket notice board
- Call a client you worked with last month to seek a case study
- Pay for an ad in a community newspaper
- Write a letter to the editor of the community newspaper
- Review how you get client feedback – and how you use it
- Write a press release
- Call the journalist you last spoke with two years ago!
- Write a grid of activity for December and January
- Identify a local geographic community to focus efforts upon
- Ensure media contacts are up to date.

# 28.
# Making a Five Year Plan

Finally, if you're not exhausted, consider writing a five year plan.

Catherine's five-year plan looked like this:

| Year | Business Requirement | Success Factors | Actions | Resources/ Finance |
|---|---|---|---|---|
| 1 | Get accredited<br><br>Gain workflow<br><br>Brand recognition<br><br>Increase cases to 37hrs/week | Solicitor referrals<br><br>Self referrals<br><br>Word of mouth<br><br>Increased income<br><br>Employ administrator | Personal introductions<br><br>Advertising<br><br>Marketing plan<br><br>Venture House office<br><br>Start online mediation | Start-up costs<br><br>Insurance, rent, memberships, training costs, etc. |

| 3 | Stable income base<br><br>Employ additional mediator<br><br>Become a PPC<br><br>Qualify for CIM | Stable income to afford additional mediator<br><br>Outgrow current office space<br><br>Pass PPC & CIM training | Move to own premises<br><br>Take PPC & CIM courses<br><br>New marketing plan | Secure income |
|---|---|---|---|---|
| 5 | Franchaise or expand brand regionally | Stable income<br><br>Recognisable brand | Promote brand/ business to other mediators<br><br>Take on self-employed mediators | Head office<br><br>Additional admin staff |

Note that the basic rule is turnover should be one and a half times your salary for you to afford to employ another mediator or staff member and continue to grow the business.

*Final TASK*

| Year | Business Requirement | Success Factors | Actions | Resources/ Finance |
|---|---|---|---|---|
| 1 | | | | |
| 3 | | | | |
| 5 | | | | |

# Appendix 1 – Business Plan

**STRATFORD**
FAMILY MEDIATION

**Name:** Stratford Family Mediation Ltd

Registered with Companies House, No. 1147014

**Domain name:**
http://stratfordfamilymediation.co.uk/com/org/net
www.stratfordfamilymediation.com

**Company Aim:** To provide a family mediation service to clients in and around Stratford-upon-Avon.

**Proposed Premises:** Venture House, Birmingham Road, Stratford-Upon-Avon CV37 0HR

Cost: £XXX per calendar month, £XXXX.00 per year inclusive of electricity, heating, water and WiFi.

https://www.venturehousestratford.co.uk/

**Business Description:** At Stratford Family Mediation, Catherine Frances will offer an affordable, personalised mediation service to clients in and around Stratford-upon-Avon who wish to divorce, separate or resolve other family conflicts quickly and efficiently.

Mediation is a voluntary and confidential process which enables both parties to explain their concerns and needs to each other in the presence of a qualified mediator (Catherine) reducing conflict by improving communication and understanding, allowing them to make informed decisions about their future.

Catherine is a qualified mediator, working towards accreditation which will take approximately 24 months. The nearby practices in Cheltenham and Worcester are not recruiting, so it is the ideal time to set up a dedicated family mediation service in south Warwickshire, although the catchment area could potentially stretch to Bourton-on-the-Water, Chipping Norton, Evesham, Redditch and Bromsgrove.

**Competitive Analysis:** There are currently no mediators offering a *family* mediation service *based* in the Stratford area. The nearest are The Worcester Family Mediation Practice in Worcester and Cheltenham Family Civil Mediation Services in Cheltenham. Halcyon Mediation in Stratford specialises in civil and commercial mediation and Family Mediation & Counselling Services are based in Nuneaton. Venture House is centrally and prominently located on the busy Birmingham Road, easily accessible by road and rail with nearby parking.

**Strengths:** Competitors' fees *start* at £XXX per hour/90 minutes/per person. Stratford Family Mediation will charge £XXX per person for each service – MIAM, 90-minute mediation session and preparation of each document. This should generate sufficient profit until demand exceeds capacity at which point prices can be increased and/or a second mediator employed. The premises allow for expansion to two mediators at no additional cost.

**Weakness:** Catherine is qualified, but working towards accreditation. This will take 24 months, at which point fees can legitimately be increased – in line with demand for services.

To address this two Professional Practice Consultants, namely XXX and XXX, have agreed to be Consultant Mediators for Stratford Family Mediation.

**Development Plan:** The proposed premises in Venture House will have capacity for up to 2 mediators working full time. Beyond this, new premises (or possibly larger office space in Venture House) will be sought. It is unlikely that the company will need to expand beyond three mediators without expanding to multiple locations.

As soon as business reaches 10 hours per week, Stratford Family Mediation Ltd will be in a position to employ a part-time administrator/receptionist.

**Financial Factors:** Catherine Frances will self-fund the start-up for the first three months, with other resources available as back-up (Business loan). In the event of incapacity: a) XXX health insurance policy will pay out b) another mediator will be employed.

One-off expenses include: creating a website and logo (£1,000.00 +VAT) and purchasing a computer and printer (£1,000.00 including VAT), plus increased marketing costs.

**Expenses:**

|  | Annual | Monthly (PCM) | Weekly |
|---|---|---|---|
| Rent** |  |  |  |
| Telephone/ Internet |  |  |  |
| Printing: Flyers, etc. Stationary |  |  |  |
| Marketing: Website Advertising |  |  |  |
| Insurance: Public liability Contents |  |  |  |
| Membership: FMA FMC Training budget |  |  |  |
| TOTAL |  |  |  |

**Including electricity, gas, heating, water, wifi, cleaning

* Estimated figures

**Budget Forecast:**

| Avg hours per week | Rate per hour | Income per week | Rent & expenses | Profit | Profit at £XXX rate per hour* |
|---|---|---|---|---|---|
| 2.5 | | | | | |
| 5 | | | | | |
| 10 | | | | | |
| 20 | | | | | |
| 25 | | | | | |
| 30 | | | | | |
| 37.5 | | | | | |

*Couples are usually charged £XXX each*

**Promotion:** Catherine is a member of the Family Mediation Council and the Family Mediators Association and therefore listed on their online registers. Stratford Family Mediation has a clear recognisable logo. Catherine will make appointments with each of the 20 law firms in Stratford to generate referrals, in addition to traditional advertising in local newspapers, bulletins and pamphlets for self-referral. The aim will be to flood the market with advertising from September to February.

- New professional logo designed.
- Professional homepage now live (weekly blog will keep it current and updated).
- A5 leaflet and business cards printed for promoting to solicitors, etc.
- Zoom backdrop designed for online mediation.

# Appendix II – Sample Invoice

**STRATFORD**
FAMILY MEDIATION

Stratford Family Mediation Ltd.
Venture House
Avenue Farm
Birmingham Road
Stratford-upon-Avon
Warwickshire
CV37 8HR
Company Number XXXXX172

## INVOICE

Bill to:                                    Invoice No.     XX01
[client name]                               Date:
                                            Due Date:

| Date | Description | | Amount |
|------|-------------|---|--------|
| | Mediation Information and Assessment Meeting | | £ |
| | 90 minute Mediation Session on Zoom | | £ |
| | | TOTAL | £ |

Please make payment to:

Account Name: Stratford Family Mediation Ltd.
Sort Code:        XX-XX-96
Account No.       XXXXX208
Bank Name:        TSB

Please remember to quote the Invoice reference number when payment is made.

# About the authors

*Richard Wyatt* has an extensive professional background in campaigns, communications and PR. In this book, Richard brings his expertise to specifically focus on the mediation profession. This will be of interest to new and experienced mediators needing to freshen up their marketing strategy. Marketing a mediation business takes a special approach, since it is an ongoing activity, as – hopefully – you don't get many repeat clients once they've reached a settlement.

*Catherine Frances* is a newly minted mediator who set up her own business from scratch, falling into every pitfall on the way! Hopefully this book will help you navigate around the traps and hazards faced by many budding mediator entrepreneurs.